GALE
CENGAGE Learning·

Epics for Students, Second Edition, Volume 2

Project Editor: Sara Constantakis Rights Acquisition and Management: Margaret Chamberlain-Gaston, Savannah Gignac, Tracie Richardson, Jhanay Williams Composition: Evi Abou-El-Seoud

Manufacturing: Drew Kalasky

Imaging: John Watkins

Product Design: Pamela A. E. Galbreath, Jennifer Wahi Content Conversion: Katrina Coach Product Manager: Meggin Condino

© 2011 Gale, Cengage Learning

ISBN-13: 978-1-4144-7621-6 (set)
ISBN-13: 978-1-4144-7622-3 (vol. 1)
ISBN-13: 978-1-4144-7623-0 (vol. 2) ISBN-10: 1-4144-7621-3 (set)
ISBN-10: 1-4144-7622-1 (vol. 1)
ISBN-10: 1-4144-7623-X (vol. 2) This title is also available as an e-book.
ISBN-13: 978-1-4144-7624-7
ISBN-10: 1-4144-7624-8
Contact your Gale, a part of Cengage Learning sales representative for ordering information.

Printed in the United States of America
1 2 3 4 5 6 7 14 13 12 11 10

Omeros

Derek Walcott

1990

Introduction

Publication of *Omeros* in 1990 signaled a milestone in the already remarkable career of Derek Walcott. This is not only because the author, who was born on the small Caribbean island of St. Lucia, went on to win the 1992 Nobel Prize for literature, but because his poem subtly undermines the very genre out of which it emerges.

Since Walcott himself voices reservations about the so-called heroic dimensions of *Omeros*, it is understandable that critics who are guided by textbook definitions have been reluctant to grant epic status to the poem. Walcott's characters are unassuming peasants who fight no monumental battles; his persona/narrator is allowed no Olympic trappings; and the requisite narrative flow is occasionally disrupted by the poem's lyrical exuberance. Nevertheless, *Omeros* is not a literary parody. The title itself pays homage to Greek origins, deriving from the pronunciation of Homer's name. Walcott's poem has the length, the geographic scope, and enough recognizable variations on traditional epic ingredients to ensure comparison with the standard masterpieces.

Indeed, the essence of Walcott's contribution to the epic genre resides in the insights afforded by that comparison. Walcott revisits the canonical works of Homer, Virgil, Dante, Milton, Walt Whitman, James Joyce, and Hart Crane because they epitomize the ideals of Western civilization. Much as Walcott admires these predecessors, he also notes that the first four reflect a world of hegemonic domination or colonialism, dividing humanity into conqueror and conquered, or marginalized *other*. Walcott's perspective is that of an artist who grew up in a neglected colony; he therefore asserts that the disenfranchised citizens of the world deserve their own validation. Whitman's *Leaves of Grass*, Joyce's *Ulysses*, and Hart Crane's *The Bridge* initiate the movement toward recognition of the common man. *Omeros* does nothing less than offer an alternative to the terms of classical heroism. *Omeros* was published by Farrar, Strauss and Giroux in 1992.

From his earliest verse written at the age of eighteen, Walcott has drawn material from his own experience. The autobiographical aspect of *Omeros* becomes unavoidable, given the frequency with which he explicitly interjects his own persona, a character with many autobiographical traits and bearing the poet's name. Furthermore, the primary subject of this poem is his native St. Lucian heritage: the rich Creole culture of his transplanted countrymen, the unfulfilled legacy of his father who died prematurely, and the all-embracing sea.

Derek and his twin brother Roderick were born to Warwick (a civil servant) and Alix Walcott (headmistress of a Methodist school) in the capital city of Castries on January 23, 1930. When the twins were about a year old, their artistically gifted father died suddenly, willing them his desire to capture the beauty of the island in the few poems and watercolors he left. Derek showed an early interest in both media. He took painting lessons from his father's friend Harold Simmons, and with a loan from his mother, privately published his first collection of verse, *25 Poems,* which he sold on the streets of Castries.

After completing his secondary schooling at St. Mary's College under English and Irish Catholic teachers, Walcott accepted a colonial development scholarship to earn his baccalaureate degree from the University of the West Indies in Jamaica, which was awarded in 1953. He taught briefly in Grenada and Jamaica before winning a Rockefeller fellowship to study theater in New York under Jose Quintero and Stuart Vaughan in 1958. The months he spent in New York were beneficial in two ways. First, they introduced him, through the examples of Bertolt Brecht's epic theater and the films of Akira Kurosawa, to the stylized technique of classical oriental drama. Second, the experience convinced him that New York in the 1950s was unreceptive to black actors and unsuitable for the kind of West Indian theater he was determined to create.

Disenchanted with prospects in the United States and armed with a new determination to succeed in the Caribbean, Walcott cut short his Rockefeller grant and settled in Port of Spain, Trinidad, in 1959. There he began writing an arts review column for the *Trinidad Guardian* while he gathered around him a group of amateur actors, dancers, musicians and stage technicians. From this highly experimental, modest beginning in the basement of a local hotel, eventually emerged the Trinidad Theatre Workshop, an institution viewed by many as the first truly professional West Indian theatrical company. The workshop gained regional and international acclaim over the years, even winning an Obie award for Walcott's *Dream on Monkey Mountain* in 1970. After he spent seventeen years of mutually rewarding collaboration, personal and artistic differences led Walcott to resign from the workshop in 1976.

After a few unsettled years of writing and mounting occasional productions as he traveled among the islands of the West Indies, Walcott accepted a series of lectureships and visiting professorships in the United States. He taught at New York University, Columbia, Harvard, Rutgers, Yale, and finally Boston University, where he remained from 1981 until well beyond his being awarded the Nobel Prize for literature in 1992; he retired from Boston University in 2007. During these years, he founded the Boston Playwrights' Theatre. Throughout this period, Walcott divided his residence between the United States and various Caribbean locations. But in 1993, he decided to build a home at Cap Estate on the northern tip of St. Lucia. After that he traveled widely, but the island was his home.

In the fall 2009, Walcott accepted a position as distinguished scholar in residence at the University of Alberta, in Canada. Then in 2010, he accepted a position as professor of poetry at the University of Essex, in Colchester, England, where he had received an honorary degree in 2008.

From the 1940s into the early 2000s, Walcott was prolific, publishing several collections of poetry each decade and over twenty plays. Among the works of poetry that appeared after *Omeros* are *Tiepolo's Hand* (2000); *The Prodigal* (2004); and *Selected Poems* (2007). Among the dramatic works following *Omeros* are 1993's *Odyssey: A Stage Version*; *The Capeman* (1997); and *Walker and the Ghost Dance* (2002).

Derek Walcott married three times, each union ending in divorce, and he fathered five children.

Plot Summary

Overview

One of the initial challenges in reading *Omeros* is the complexity of its multi-layered plot. Themeaning of the epic builds on events that are straightforward within themselves. Simple fishermen Achille (pronounced A-sheel) and Hector fight over Helen, awoman they both desire. Walcott expands these basic parts so that Helen comes to personify an island nation historically coveted by European powers. While his narrative does move toward an end, Walcott is essentially interested in the journey itself. Indeed, the nearer he comes to the final resolution, the more he focuses on the act of writing. Given his conscious emphasis on the text of the poem as one of his subjects, his epic becomes selfreflexive.

Media Adaptations

- Excerpts from Walcott's *Omeros*, the *Odyssey*, and *Collected Poems* are read by the author on a Caedmon audiotape, recorded November 18, 1993, and available from Harper Collins Publishers.

- Walcott reads excerpts from *Omeros* and discusses the epic in a 1991 taped interview with Rebekah Presson, released as "Derek Walcott" in the *New Letters on the Air: Contemporary Writers on Radio* series, available from the University of Missouri in Kansas City.

- Derek Walcott reads his poems "Blues" and "Sea Canes" in an Audio Workshop London recording made by Richard Carrington on June 5, 2007. The recording can be heard online.

- Derek Walcott was recorded reading his poems at Calabash '08, the international literary festival at Treasure Beach, Jamaica, on May 24, 2008. The recording is available online.

Omeros is a story of homecoming comprised

of seven books recounting a circular journey that ends where it begins. Books one and two introduce St. Lucia and key sets of characters and initiate the basic conflicts. Books three, four, and five retrace the triangular trade route that once linked Europe, Africa, and the Americas. Books six and seven return to St. Lucia where the wandering author and his uprooted countrymen are eventually reconciled to their Creole identity.

Book One

The primary focus of the first book is a group of indigenous fishermen and their friends in Gros Ilet village. Philoctete entertains a group of tourists willing to pay to hear local lore and to photograph the gruesome scar on his shin. Philoctete's tale, like that of his Greek namesake Philoctetes, goes back to the cause of his old wound and his quest for a cure. Two of Philoctete's companions, Achille and Hector, have ended their friendship fighting over Helen, while Helen herself has broken with Achille, the man she loves and, out of spite, has moved in with Hector. Pregnant by one of these rivals and out of work, she is, like her counterpart Helen of Troy, caught between two jealous contenders. Rounding out the central cast of peasants are the old blind sailor, Omeros, also known as "Seven Seas," and Ma Kilman, proprietress of the No Pain Cafe. Omeros in different manifestations serves as a wise seer, an interested commentator on the fate of others, and ultimately as the incarnation of the Greek epic poet Homer himself. Ma Kilman serves as a medicine woman, interested in a folk cure for Philoctete's suffering.

Another equally important set of characters includes the persona of the author himself, whose fictionalized character moves in and out of the story to recount his autobiographical journey toward self-realization. On a social level comparable with the author's persona is the white, expatriate couple Major Dennis Plunkett and his wife Maud Plunkett. As Walcott's persona puts it in one of his earliest incursions into the plot, each of his characters is wounded in one way or another because "affliction is one theme of this work," and he goes on to admit candidly that "every 'I,';" including the narrator's own, "is a fiction."

Achille, Hector, Walcott, and Plunkett all seek to possess Helen. Walcott makes her, as the personification of St. Lucia, the object of his epic. Alienated as Dennis and Maud are on their adopted island, their deepest regret is that they have no heir. To occupy his mind, it occurs to the major that Helen and her neglected people deserve to have their story recorded. To Plunkett's allusive imagination, correspondences between the Trojan war and the protracted Anglo-French battle to dominate St. Lucia, the Helen of the West Indies, are too close to be merely coincidental. As persona Walcott and Plunkett undertake their writing projects, Achille agonizes over Helen's defection to Hector, while Hector suspects that Helen still loves Achille.

Book one concludes with an episode that may

be seen as a reversal of Major Plunkett's longing for a son. Walcott, the poet, regretted not having a father. In the final scene, the ghost of Warwick Walcott materializes to encourage his son to complete his unfinished work. He urges his son to honor their nameless ancestors, all the overlooked Helens, the female colliers who marched like black ants down to visiting steamers—"to give those feet a voice."

Book Two

The second book centers on two major events, each affecting one of the groups of characters already introduced. The first event involves the historical 1782 sea battle that ensured British sovereignty over St. Lucia. Leading up to his retelling of the Battle of the Saints, Walcott takes readers back to meet a young midshipman on a spy mission for British Admiral George Brydges Rodney in a distant Dutch port two hundred years earlier. Next he shifts across the Atlantic to witness Rodney's simultaneous preparations for the defense of St. Lucia. Rodney singles out for recognition one of the slaves struggling to transport a cannon up the coastal bluffs. These two new figures fill ancestral blanks for Major Plunkett and Achille: The ill-fated young midshipman entrusted with the Dutch mission is named Plunkett. When Dennis discovers his surname among dusty island archives, he claims the son he has always wanted. The slave, Afolabe, whom Rodney distinguished with the Greek name Achilles, is an ancestor of Achille. These preliminaries out of the way, a flashback describes the Battle of the Saints and Midshipman Plunkett's untimely death. At the moment that the French ship *Ville de Paris* broadsides Plunkett's vessel *Marlborough*, the midshipman accidentally falls on his own unsheathed sword.

The second of the pivotal episodes of this book involves a political campaign sweeping the newly independent island. Philoctete and Hector join Maljo's fledgling United Love Party. Maljo points to lame Philoctete as a symbol of the infirm status of the nation. Hector, who has given up the sea to convey passengers around the island in his van, the Comet, provides transportation. Maljo's get-out-the-vote extravaganza is rained out, and after defeat, the candidate retreats to Florida to work the citrus harvest. The point of this interlude is to note that the transition from imperial rule to self-government has not improved the life of the average citizen. As Major Plunkett observes, local politicians have not helped Philoctete and have not affected the price Ma Kilman pays for fuel. Hector's remaking himself into a taxi driver has been equally ineffectual. Closing book two, Achille puts out to sea, where the sun induces hallucinatory visions. As Achille's fantasy begins, he sees past generations of drowned men rising to the surface. These remnants of the Middle Passage conjure vestiges of his enslaved forefathers. As his fishing boat, the pirogue named *In God We Troust* heads toward his lost African home, Achille considers for the first time the question of his identity.

Book Three

The actual time span covered in book three is approximately twenty-four hours, but in his trance, Achille retraces the Middle Passage back across centuries and vast distances to his ancestral African village. There he encounters his grandsire Afolabe, who instructs him in his forgotten tribal identity. In the local dances, rituals, tools, and musical instruments, Achille recognizes the origins of St. Lucian customs and devices. Together Afolabe and the village griot, or storyteller, rectify the historic amnesia of the African diaspora. Dream turns to nightmare, however, as Achille is forced to stand by helplessly as tribal enemies raid his village for slaves.

Meanwhile, *In God We Troust* does not return at dusk with the rest of the pirogues. Philoctete and Helen wait anxiously until the next day for Achille. Back in St. Lucia, he acquires a new interest in the fates of dispossessed Native Americans and Africans in the New World. Bob Marley's song "Buffalo Soldier," heard on the radio, subtly broadens Achille's perspective and, at the same time, offers a foretaste of the setting for the fourth book.

Book Four

Time and space are once again divided in the fourth book. It includes scenes set in present-day New England, where Walcott suffers over the failure of his marriage and a visit to the Dakota Indian territories in the 1890s. There, the Oglala Lakota Sioux are reacting to the genocidal policies of white men by joining the Ghost Dance, a millenarian religious movement of Plains tribes. Participation in the Ghost Dance alarmed officials monitoring activities on the reservations and led to the massacre of more than three hundred families camped along Wounded Knee Creek on the Pine Ridge reservation in South Dakota on December 29, 1890. The dominant point of view for this sequence of events is that of the historical figure Catherine Weldon. Weldon, a wealthy white woman from New York, resembles the Plunketts of the main narrative in that she is both emblematic of her race and at the same time has voluntarily broken with her own race and class in order to identify with people who have been deprived of their place in history. In a scene mirroring the aftermath of the slave raid in Afolabe's village, Weldon stands, helpless as Achille had been, listening to the shaman Seven Seas recite the litany of an Indian village wiped out by cavalrymen.

Inevitably, Walcott identifies with Weldon. As she watches the blanketing snow eradicate traces of disappearing Native Americans, he watches the snow wipe out familiar landmarks around his Boston townhouse. While he contemplates the breach of man-made treaties—government documents to wedding vows—the ghost of Warwick Walcott reappears to instruct him that his odyssey, like all journeys, is circular. Before Walcott can go back to his tropical island, however, his father urges him to experience the metropolitan capitals of the Old World that have influenced and shaped his colonial culture.

Book Five

Europe has always been more than just the seat of imperial domination to Walcott: The poet's ancestry and that of his persona in the epic include a mixture of Dutch and English forebears in his grandparents' generation. When the poet's persona Walcott crosses the Atlantic this time, he selects four destinations that hold special significance. First is Lisbon, Portugal, early patron of the African slave trade, and once so powerful that (in 1493) Pope Alexander VI allotted it half the unexplored world. Second is London, England, the colonial administrator and source of the language Walcott, the poet, has treasured since birth. Third is Dublin, Ireland, the island immortalized by his childhood idol, James Joyce, and Maud Plunkett's native country. The fourth destination is the Aegean islands, the birthplace of Western culture. From his examination of the grand monuments of the past, Walcott concludes that he prefers "not statues, but the bird in the statue's hair." In other words, although he continues to be influenced by the established literary canon, he wishes to draw material from the life around him, just as Homer and Joyce did.

Book Six

By the sixth book, Walcott has made his return to

St. Lucia and it remains for him to gather the strands of his converging plots. After depicting the wreck of the Comet in which Hector is killed, Walcott is guided to the site by a talkative taxi driver. Next, Ma Kilman follows a trail of ants into the mountains and retrieves the homeopathic African herb that finally cures Philoctete's open wound. As Philoctete is cleansed, Walcott catalogs the terms of his healing. His flesh and spirit are restored as his racial shame is washed away and he reclaims his lost name.

Similarly, Walcott exorcizes the flaw in his love of St. Lucia. His artistic preservation of local color does no justice to the integrity of living people. Soon afterward, Major Plunkett achieves a similar change of heart. His epiphany dawns shortly after his wife Maud dies from cancer. Walcott sums up their mutual conversion when he denounces the grandiose classical trappings in their homage to Helen: "Why not see Helen as the sun saw her, with no Homeric shadow?"

Nearing the end of *Omeros* the announced theme of affliction gradually yields to the theme of reconciliation. Not only is every *I* a fictional construct, but each is easily interchangeable. Walcott invests his father in Plunkett, his mother in Maud, and he sees himself as a Telemachus launching his own odyssey in search of his missing Odysseus. The father/son variations proliferate. History may have shaped the present, but nothing prevents the individual from adjusting the perception of present and future options. At Maud's funeral, Helen informs Achille that she is coming home. As this sixth book concludes, Achille helps Helen understand the insights of his African dream: The costumes, dances, and rituals celebrating Boxing Day (the day following Christmas) have roots that descend through Western customs into African origins. In their Creole practice, they now inform St. Lucian identity.

Book Seven

The Protean Omeros materializes as an animated statue in the seventh book to assure Walcott that a real "girl smells better than the world's libraries" therefore, he should concentrate on what he sees around him. Walcott resolves to emulate the sea that absorbs history and to appreciate the privilege of knowing "a fresh people." Helen is no longer the object of an agenda for Walcott or Major Plunkett. The major accepts Maud's death and learns to work among rather than to oversee his employees. Achille, who will never read anything Walcott writes, is depicted returning from a day of fishing, and the final line of the epic notes that "the sea was still going on."

Characters

Achille

The primary protagonist among the villagers of Gros Ilet in St. Lucia, Achille (pronounced Asheel) is a fisherman deeply in love with Helen, the local beauty. Because he and his friend Hector both love Helen, they become arch-rivals, as did their Homeric namesakes three thousand years earlier. Afflicted with the rootlessness that often results from living under colonialism, Achille not only needs towin Helen, he also must discover his personal and racial roots in order to confirm his rightful place in St. Lucia. The event that gives his life ultimate meaning is a sunstroke-induced trance that transports him through time and space to his ancestral river village in Africa.

Achilles

See Achille

Afolabe

In the dream that takes Achille centuries back to his African origins, Afolabe appears as his distant grandsire. Afolabe challenges Achille to reclaim his African name, believing that the person who forgets who he is lacks the substance to cast his own shadow. Under Afolabe's instruction, the amnesia caused by the Middle Passage and generations of slavery is eliminated. Achille is surprised to see familiar traces of St. Lucian rituals in Afolabe's tribal customs.

Anti gone

The Greek sculptress who instructs Walcott in the proper pronunciation of Omeros (Homer's name) is given the pseudonym Anti gone. She appears briefly as Walcott's lover in her Boston studio in book one. She disappears almost at once because she has grown tired of the United States and wants to return to her native islands.

Christine

Christine is Ma Kilman's niece, a country girl who comes to work in the No Pain Cafe at the end of *Omeros*. For her, Gros Ilet is an amazing city and she is said to be like a new Helen.

Chrysostom

Chrysostom is one of the fishermen who gather with Achille and others on the shore before beginning work each day.

Circe

See Helen

F. Didier

Convinced that there is no significant difference between the two major parties that are polarizing the island in attempting to win the general elections, Maljo creates his alternative United Love party. Maljo runs an ineffective, American-style, grass-roots campaign, driving along the streets, shouting through an unreliable megaphone about Greek and Trojan parties fighting over Helen. When Maljo is defeated, he leaves for Florida to work the citrus harvests.

Hector

Achille's friend turned rival, Hector manages to take Helen home with him early in *Omeros,* buthe suffers from knowing that he has not won her heart. Hector's downfall is the result of his turning away from the calling of the sea to become a taxi driver. His van named the Comet, decorated with flames on the outside and leopard-skin upholstery within, symbolizes the island's cultural ambiguity. The leopard motif harks back to an Africa that no longer exists, while the blazing comet suggests an alluring future driven by tourism and corporate exploitation far beyond local control. Once he abandons the sea, Hector is never at peace, and he can find no security in Helen. In the sixth book, reckless driving takes him over a cliff to his death. Despite Hector's treachery in life, Achille mourns for an irreplaceable friend. Walcott shows Hector last shouldering an oar as a road-warrior in the inferno section of the seventh book, a soul in the purgatory of his own choosing.

Helen

Helen is the cause of the conflict between Achille and Hector. Walcott, as a participating narrator, is inspired to immortalize her in *Omeros*. In spite of all the Homeric paraphernalia surrounding her, Walcott insists on her existence as a real person. As he explained to J. P. White, Helen is based on a woman he saw in a transport van he described in the poem "The Light of the World."

James Joyce

When Walcott stops in Dublin on his tour of Europe, he pays homage to James Joyce. As he stands on the embankment of the Liffey River one evening, he imagines Joyce's Anna Livia (from *Finnegans Wake*) scurrying by. Then he conjures up the image of Joyce (with his notoriously poor eyesight) as a "one-eyed Ulysses" gazing seaward after a departing ship.

Ma Kilman

Ma Kilman is the repository of African animism that has been adopted into St. Lucia's Catholicism through generations of obeah-women (practitioners of sorcery and magic with roots in African traditions). She has lost the memory of herbs, potions, and spells, but when she sheds the uncomfortable garments of civilization, she reestablishes contact with the homeopathic fruit of the earth. Ma Kilman serves as an earth-mother figure, healing men and linking them with the natural environment.

Lawrence

The waiter having difficulty making his way among customers on the beach when both Walcott and the Plunketts observe Helen's first appearance in *Omeros* is sarcastically called "Lawrence of St. Lucia." He is no Lawrence of Arabia. Near the end of the epic Walcott mentions his name once again as an example of the "wounded race" who laugh uncomprehendingly when an exasperated Achille curses a group of intrusive tourists.

Maljo

See F. Didier

St. Omere

See Omeros

Omeros

The title character is an ageless blind man who has settled in St. Lucia after sailing the oceans of the world. Omeros, like both the island's sightless patron St. Lucia and the Greek Homer, possesses the gift of inner vision.

Pancreas

Pancreas is one of the fishermen who gather with Achille and others on the shore before beginning work each day.

Penelope

See Helen

Philo

See Philoctete

Philoctete

Philoctete serves as an integral mediator. He tries to convince Achille and Hector that they are brothers in the bond of the sea and should not be estranged from each other. When budding political parties in his newly independent nation threaten to divide the population against itself, he regrets the fact that people do not love St. Lucia as a whole.

Philosophe

See Philoctete

Placide

Placide is one of the fishermen who gather with Achille and others on the shore before beginning work each day.

Major Dennis Plunkett

Expatriate Dennis Plunkett, a retired British major, settled in St. Lucia with his wife Maud shortly after World War II. He sustained a head wound in the war, and Maud nursed him back to health. As Walcott informs the reader in one of his earliest authorial intrusions, the major's injury is in keeping with the epic's central theme of affliction. At first glance, this white, landowning couple seems out of place among the predominantly black islanders. Their presence, however, may be justified on at least two counts. First, they represent the centuries-old European entanglements in St. Lucian affairs. Second, Walcott's identification of the Plunketts with his parents recognizes the European blood in his own veins. The deepest regret in Dennis Plunkett's life is that he and his wife never had a son.

Maud Plunkett

Maud Plunkett, the wife of Dennis Plunkett, longs for the music and the seasonal changes of her native Ireland. Much as she would like to see her homeland once again, her husband will not spare the money for passage. Maud is a static character, the steady anchor to her husband's often quixotic energy. Dennis refers to her as his "crown," his "queen."

Midshipman Plunkett

Midshipman Plunkett serves two primary functions in *Omeros*. In an historical flashback, Midshipman Plunkett is entrusted by Admiral Rodney with a spy mission to Dutch ports to gather information on the enemies of England. Unfortunately, he dies later by accidentally falling on his own sword after his ship is breached in the Battle of the Saints. His second, more important, role is to lie dormant for two hundred years before his name is rediscovered, allowing him to become the surrogate son Major Dennis Plunkett thought he would never have. The major uses the midshipman imaginatively to link his ancestry with his adopted home of St. Lucia. It does not matter that the young man died centuries before Dennis was born; the event allows the major to take pride in the actions of a namesake who died honorably in defense of the Helen of the West Indies.

Admiral Rodney

Commander of the British fleet stationed in Gros Ilet Bay in the eighteenth century, the historical Admiral George Brydges Rodney defeated the French fleet under the Count de Grasse on April 12, 1782. The Battle of the Saints, named for the small group of Les Saintes islands, is famous in naval history because Rodney's bold breaking-of-the-line maneuver established precedent for future naval engagements, and his victory solidified the British position in peace negotiations with France.

In book two of *Omeros*, Admiral Rodney

dispatches Midshipman Plunkett to spy on the Dutch. He is also responsible for changing the African name of Achille's ancestor Afolabe to Achilles.

La Sorciere

See Ma Kilman

Seven Seas

See Omeros

Professor Static

See F. Didier

Statics

See F. Didier

Theophile

Theophile is one of the fishermen who gather with Achille and others on the shore before beginning work each day.

Alix Walcott

Alix Walcott, the aged mother of Derek Walcott, appears only once in *Omeros*, but Walcott makes the comment that she is incorporated into his portrayal of Maud Plunkett. Derek Walcott, the poet's persona, visits her at a nursing home where she resides.

The domestic scene in which Walcott meets Alix is a respite from the constantly shifting narrative. Walcott must prompt his mother, who struggles to remember the names of her loved ones. She finally recalls "Derek, Roddy, and Pam," the children she bore Warwick. The scene reconfirms Walcott's roots in the island before he must be off again, pursuing a calling that takes him away from the source of his inspiration.

Derek Walcott

Derek Walcott, the persona of the poet, functions in *Omeros* on two primary levels. He expresses fascination with Helen, enters into dialogue, and is often a participant among groups of characters. In addition, he candidly discusses autobiographical details and discloses the underlying structure of *Omeros* as he is engaged in the writing process. Despite the apparent transparency of motive, however, it would be a grave error to conclude that the Walcott who appears in *Omeros* is identical to the Walcott who is the author of the text. The persona is a fictional construct, an element in the epic that serves the poet's artistic purposes; thus, the persona is distinct from the poet who wrote the epic.

Warwick Walcott

Warwick Walcott, the actual father of the poet

Derek Walcott, was an influence on his son's artistic ambitions, despite having died when his son was only a little child. This fact accounts for the two pivotal appearances of the persona of Warwick's ghost in *Omeros*, and it also serves the father/son relationships that proliferate in the epic. Warwick appears first at the end of book one to focus Derek's attention on events of the past and present in the city of his birth. The ghost of Warwick materializes a second time at the conclusion of the fourth book, catching his son in a period of depression over his broken marriage and life in Boston. At this juncture, Warwick advises his son to follow the example of the sea-swift and complete his odyssey by circling back home.

Catherine Weldon

The historical Catherine Weldon was a widow from New York whose commitment to the cause of Native Americans led her to the Indian territories of the Dakotas in the 1890s. Walcott's treatment of her as a fictional persona seems to be faithful to historical and biographical accounts. Weldon became private secretary to Sitting Bull during the time that the Ghost Dance movement was making its way through the plains tribes, creating uneasiness among white settlers and frontier military units. The Ghost Dance offered the Sioux the false promise that the vanishing buffalo herds and past generations of Native American warriors would return. The Sioux also believed that the magic shirts worn during the dance rituals would render their wearers invulnerable to bullets. White frontiersmen feared the unifying, rallying force of the movement and used the unrest it caused among Anglo Americans as an excuse for the Wounded Knee Creek massacre of 1890.

Themes

Hegemony and Identity

On several levels, *Omeros* presents the strategies by which human beings survive and assert their integrity despite overwhelming hegemonic forces. Walcott's peasant fishermen of Gros Ilet suffer neglect and shame because imperial power has deprived them of their ancestral culture. Expatriate residents of St. Lucia Dennis Plunkett and Maud Plunkett must adapt in order to exist in a marginalized colony. In a reversal of the standard paternalistic relationship between metropolis and colony, Walcott introduces several father-son combinations that are liberating and mutually beneficial. Last, the author uses vestiges of the epic literary tradition to assert a basis for self-esteem, even heroism, among dispossessed people, while he simultaneously challenges the very artistic form through which he makes his assertion.

Affliction, Deprivation, and Self-Esteem

Walcott mentions early in *Omeros* that "affliction is one theme of this work." Philoctete already has a seemingly incurable wound on his shin, and Major Dennis Plunkett has sustained a head injury. Walcott makes it clear, however, that this theme operates on a figurative level as well. Philoctete, for example, traces the persistence of his open sore to the chains that shackled his enslaved grandfathers. The major is tormented by his feelings that, like the history and people of his adopted colonial home, unfairly pushed to the margins of history, his own name and fame will die with him because he has no heir. Achille's afflictions include both the pain in his heart over his loss of Helen and the amnesia he suffers in having been cut off from his cultural roots. Given the dimensions of such wounds, it follows that the cures must necessarily be complex. Philoctete is restored to health when Ma Kilman rediscovers an herb and the homeopathic remedies of her ancient African grandmothers. In order to regain his soul, Achille must be transported in a dream back to the African village from which his ancestors were kidnapped into slavery hundreds of years earlier. Later, when Achille accepts his identity as a transplanted man of the New World, Helen returns, and he can begin to help her to understand the African roots that now draw nourishment from St. Lucian soil. The major gradually learns to feel whole and to make a place for himself. Helen figures prominently in his quest in the role he has imposed on her as the personification of the island of St. Lucia. Dennis Plunkett decides to rectify history's negligence toward Helen and her people by dedicating himself to writing her history. His subsequent research into the Battle of the Saints fortuitously provides the name of Midshipman Plunkett as his putative son. The young man may have died in the conflict, but the crucial value of the major's discovery is that it gives him a blood tie to St. Lucia. Later, after his wife dies, his attachment to the local people is confirmed as Ma Kilman helps him to feel even closer to Maud than he did when she was alive.

Topics for Further Study

- Dennis Plunkett, a British expatriate, feels a greater sense of belonging to his adopted community of St. Lucia after he discovers that a possible ancestor of his died in its defense. Identify and write about an actual historical case of amember of another race or culture dying or risking death in the defense of a land, people, or cause not his or her own.

- As political leaders discovered in the years following the American

Revolution of 1776, the requirements for achieving independence extend far beyond a declaration, awar, and the formation of a national government. There are challenges of cultural, economic, psychological, and social independence as well. Conduct research into the post-revolutionary period of the United States. Compare the obstacles that had to be overcome with those faced in modern times by a nation such as St. Lucia, newly emerged from colonialism since World War II. In a PowerPoint presentation, explore the similarities and differences between the nature of independence seeking in U.S. history and that of a country seeking independence in the early 2000s.

- Although sophisticated forms of art may seem to be detached from the real world, Walcott recognizes that art can serve as a valuable means of human expression. Investigate some of the folk arts, crafts, dance, music, or rituals of Africans or Native Americans. Determine ways that these media help people to identify and define themselves as a culture. Create a poster on which you display scanned images you found in the library or online, showing these media and how they convey identity.

- Do online research on the art, literature, film, or music that has been produced by colonized people in a country occupied by military forces from another country. Make a presentation to your class that explains the concept of hegemony and incorporates examples of the creative work of an oppressed people and discuss how the art conveys the feelings of those who are oppressed.

- Research a current and ongoing instance of an outside power that is exploiting natural resources in a foreign country for economic reasons. Write a research paper in which you explain how multinational companies or foreign governments are able to take over and profit from the natural resources that exist in other countries. Or write a biographical portrait of a person who has devoted his or her life to defending native rights and resisting outside powerful interests.

Colonialism and Independence

One of the many unfortunate legacies of colonial domination is that subject peoples are likely to learn to value themselves and their colony according to the standards of their subjugators. In *Omeros*, Walcott registers this fact in terms of psychological, sociological, political, and cultural effects, which explains why he begins his epic with deliberate classical allusions and launches his odyssey to North America and Europe in books four and five. The gesture, however, leaves the poet qpen to charges of imitation. This unavoidable influence is also what prompts Major Plunkett to champion Helen's cause by attempting to match Eurocentric history. Achille's journey to Africa gives him back his name and depicts his justified pride in his origins, but his most valuable insight is that Africa is not his home. His ancestors "crossed, they survived. There is the epical splendour ... the grace born from subtraction." Philoctete's involvement in Maljo's abortive political campaign underscore's the internecine strife that threatens a newly independent nation experimenting with democracy.

However, self-determination all too obviously does not guarantee cultural independence. One of the most insidious vestiges of neo-colonialism is tourism. Beautiful tropical havens attract so many leisure transients that national economies become vulnerable to foreign priorities. Reacting to the changes being wrought in St. Lucia by modernizing entrepreneurs, Walcott's persona begins to suspect his own relationship with the island. Near the end of the poem, the influx of tourists and corporate interests drives Achille and Philoctete to undertake a voyage in search of an unspoiled island where they can begin anew. Eventually they recognize that they must return, proclaim their integrity, and defend their native home despite its remaining under duress.

Art and Reality

One of the pervasive themes that begins early and grows to paramount importance in the last two books concerns Walcott's self-reflexive point of view in *Omeros*. Walcott names his poem after Homer, the wandering poet who is credited with writing down the oral versions of the Greek epics and thus establishing an epic tradition, and Walcott incorporates elements of the epic genre in order to sustain parallels and create contrasts. Since his intention is to validate a corner of the world that past individuals considered unimportant, he must ultimately negate expected terms of heroism and advance a new perspective. He creates room to maneuver when he first insists that every *I* is a fiction. Doing so allows him to invest some aspect of himself in one after another of his characters. Such candor also disrupts the artifice of his text and thins the separation between art and its creator. It allows readers to have the sense that they can be privy to the poet's intentions. Walcott's persona and Major Plunkett start out together in asserting their West Indian Helen's right to capitalize on certain coincidental Greek and Trojan parallels. But both of them come to understand that by molding Helen into the object of their imaginative designs, they do an injustice to the actual woman, who has a right to be no more nor less than just herself. In keeping with every imperial conqueror before them, they were exploiting a resource for their own gain. Gradually *Omeros* begins to dismantle the artistic structure in order to unmask the reality that is its inspiration. After having been impressed by the monuments dedicated to European conquistadors in the fifth book, Walcott expresses a preference not for the statues, "but for the bird in the statue's hair," meaning not the art object but the life that surrounds it. He advances another step when in the next book he comes to realize that as an artist he is guilty of wanting to preserve in his imagery the quaint world of the poor. He concludes that "Art is History's nostalgia," sacrificing the real for the ideal. Yet he chooses to write about Achille, who would never care to read his own story. Walcott's answer, typically metaphorical, is twofold. First, the illiterate sea, which never reads the epics of mankind is still its own "epic where every line was erased *yet freshly written in sheets of exploding surf." Second, Achille's race, like living coral that builds on itself, "a quiet culture* is branching from the white ribs of each ancestor." Finally he speaks through Major Plunkett when he decides to let Helen be herself, the reality on which the sun shines naturally, for "she was not a cause or a cloud, only a name /for a local wonder."

Form serves function in *Omeros* as forces of hegemonic power, deprivation, colonial neglect, and paternalistic literary influences come under the scrutiny of an artist from the third world, who records his people's struggle to establish their identity and reclaim their self-esteem and independence even while he questions his own artistic processes.

Epic Features

Although *Omeros* resembles canonical epics in many ways, Walcott purposely deviates from the genre in order to broaden the scope of this traditionally heroic form. The lengthy though not consistently elevated poetic language is often more lyrical than narrative. There is no attempt to appear objective and the protagonists range from a persona of the poet himself to simple peasants who are the opposite of the Greek demigods whom Homer depicted. There is an effort to establish identity and a greater sense of nationhood, along with a validation of personal and national history apart from or despite colonization. Similarly, Walcott depends on frequent allusions to and parallels with Homer, Virgil, Dante, and others in order to place his work within and oppose his work to canonical epics. But in the end, his goal is to validate simple men and women whose very survival requires heroic action, and not to claim for them any connection to supernatural forces or spiritual realms.

Point of View

Because Walcott makes one of his protagonists a persona very much based on his own personality and history, his perspective is always at hand within the epic he creates. Under other circumstances his insinuating his own views through a mouthpiece might undermine the individuality of other characters; however, in this case, Walcott uses a self-reflexive technique, candidly insisting that each narrative voice, or *I*, is a fiction, including his own. This is a crucial point, considering that one of his purposes is to dramatize the fact that all accounts of events, whether in an epic poem or a so-called factual history, are selective narratives or constructs. The controlling voice determines what is central and what is relegated to the margins. In this sense, then, Walcott shifts the subject and range of focus from the center (heroic) to the margin (common), thus privileging what would in a traditional epic be treated as minor and demoting what in a traditional epic would be center. Given this shift, then, through his persona he is able to create a new version of epic, one that celebrates the individual and deconstructs the concept of conquest. Too, he is able to comment on roles played within the text hewrites.

Setting

The main action takes place in postcolonial St. Lucia, in the United States, and in certainmajor European capitals. Historically, the West Indies have been shaped by the influx of alien races and cultures; therefore, theepic plot telescopesbackward in time to resurrect and interpret anew certain past events that affected the present. Ina vision, Achille is transported three hundred years into the past to recover forgotten African rituals and witness tribesmen being captured by members of their own race for sale into slavery. Other episodes include the Battle of the Saints from 1782 and incidents from the 1890s in the American frontier. The story follows Walcott, a persona of the poet, as he travels from St. Lucia to Boston, to Europe, and back to the Caribbean. Since all the events have psychological repercussions for various characters, much of the action is internal, as each resolves personal problems.

Allusions

From the very beginning, *Omeros* depends on readers recognizing and seeing the present significance in numerous allusions to certain canonical epics. The title refers to Homer and is a version of his name, and many of the characters' names echo leading figures from the *Iliad* and *Odyssey*. In addition, in his historical research, Major Plunkett finds parallels between the Trojan War and the Battle of the Saints. Aside from the classical and historical allusions, Walcott also makes reference to certain subsequent authors, painters, and sculptors as he explores the manner by which he and other artists translate their reality into art.

Imagery

Walcott makes extensive use of sensory perception throughout *Omeros*. The pronunciation of Omeros' name is replicated in the "O" sound of the blown conch shell. The blind Omeros perceives his environment by ear. Walcott and his fellow fishermen relate to the sea as mother, *mer* in their patois, and her surf writes and erases her message all along the shoreline of their island. Birds proliferate on Maud Plunkett's tapestry and the sea-swift becomes a focal point for several characters, both literally and figuratively. Philoctete's existence is virtually defined by his painful wound. Helen's beauty, her proud bearing, and her signature yellow dress turn heads where ever she appears. Aside from these standard appeals to the senses, Walcott's text draws attention to itself or is self-reflexive. He mentions his thought of a Crow horseman taking shape as he inscribes it in book four then in the fifth book falling snow and the whiteness of the physical page are conflated with "the obliteration *of nouns fading into echoes, the alphabet* of scribbling branches."

Symbolism

The sea surrounds the island, connects this place with distant continents, and serves as the source of the fishermen's sustenance. It also symbolizes the historical amnesia afflicting St. Lucia's native population. Generations of African emigrants have forgotten their roots, just as each wave line left on the shore is erased by its successor. Time and again these ancestors are seen, for example, as a line of worker ants, toiling under the weight of their burdens. The sea-swift in flight makes the sign of the cross against the sky; it leads Achille's pirogue on his African odyssey. The ghost of Warwick Walcott cites the swift's habitual flight pattern, seaward and back, as the model his son must follow in order to trace his way back to St. Lucia. Wounds within each character symbolize the afflictions attendant upon slavery, colonialism, and metropolitan subjugation. Ma Kilman's homeopathic cure of Philoctete serves as baptism into a new life, freeing him to remember the past without any longer being its victim. The journey motifs—whether in dreams of Africa or of Soufriere's Malebolge; whether they are the poet's personal sojourns to the United States and Europe; whether to connect the present with Greece, the Battle of the Saints, or the American Dakotas—all are diverse paths leading to wholeness for Walcott's protagonists.

Prosody

The basic poetic structure of *Omeros* is occasionally off-rhymed terza rima stanzas. The rhyme scheme often interlocks, as is expected of terza rima, but Walcott ranges from exact to many forms of off-rhyme. On rare occasions, there are couplets and tetrameter passages. Walcott described his meter as "roughly hexametrical" the "roughly" needs emphasis. The numbers of loose iambic feet vary to the extent that the stanzas often approximates free verse.

Helen of the West Indies

The setting of *Omeros* ranges from the past to the late 1990s in the Caribbean, Africa, North America, and Europe, but the constant center is Walcott's native island of St. Lucia. St. Lucia is the second largest of the Windward group of the Lesser Antilles. Small and insignificant as it may appear among so many islands, it has a remarkably colorful history. The population in 1990 was 151,000, comprised of 90.3 percent African descent, mixed (5.5%), East Indian (3.2%), and European (0.8%). Early attempts at European settlement were undertaken in the sixteenth century. Largely because of its strategic location and its fine harbors, St. Lucia rapidly became a pawn in Europe's imperial expansion. The island was passed between England and France fourteen times before it was finally ceded to England by the Treaty of Paris in 1814. As a result of the protracted martial and legal contention, St. Lucia has been called the Gibraltar of the Caribbean and the Helen of the West Indies. Agricultural products have been the main source of revenue—first sugar and then bananas. Until the advent of petroleum-fueled ships in the late 1920s locally mined coal was important in the economy.

Despite the fact that the official language has been English since 1842, a majority of the population continues to speak a French patois, and 90 percent are Roman Catholic. This is the milieu in which Derek Walcott, an educated, middle-class, artistically gifted member of a Methodist family, grew to adulthood. Walcott contended with white grandfathers and black grandmothers on both sides of his family and the untimely death of his father. Walcott struggled to find himself with few established guidelines. As he expressed it in his 1972 autobiographical poem *Another Life*, "The dream *of reason had produced its monster;* a prodigy of the wrong age and colour." As a student, he was impressed with the poetry of Guadeloupe-born Saint-John Perse (pseudonym of Alexis Saint-Leger Leger), but his own early verse and dramatic work reflect the British colonial educational influences of the metaphysical poets and of Milton, John Millington Synge, T. S. Eliot, James Joyce, and Dylan Thomas. Later he added traces of Kipling, Conrad, and Hemingway, then writers who became personal friends, including Robert Lowell, Joseph Brodsky, and Seamus Heaney. Regardless of the number of Western masters he may have assimilated, Walcott remained constant in his determination to draw from the most immediate subject matter of his life, the confluence of disparate cultures in the West Indies.

The Middle Passage

The Middle Passage refers to the forcible removal of Africans from their native homes and their inhumane transport across the Atlantic Ocean in slave ships to live out their lives as slaves on plantations in the New World. Because Caribbean islands were populated by slaves and because part of Walcott's own heritage is African, the Middle Passage is of central importance. For these reasons, the poet decided to send Achille back three hundred years, across the Middle Passage on a dream quest to eliminate the amnesia and the shame inflicted by the history of Western subjugation. Treated as merchandise and dispersed without regard to family ties or place of origin, forced to give up their language, religion, customs, and true names, slaves were able to retain and pass down only fragments of their African identity. Walcott treats Achille's indoctrination as instinctive or racial memory. In the primitive dress, instruments, and rituals, he detects traces of ancient African practices he only partially understands given his St. Lucian socialization. When he has Achille observe one African tribe abduct members of another to be sold into slavery, Walcott dramatizes the fact that man's inhumanity to man knows no racial boundaries. Walcott is careful not to imply that Achille's knowledge of tribal life makes him somehow become African. It is important to him that Achille reclaim this part of his past and incorporate it into his authentic identity as a West Indian, an integral member of a Creole culture. Toward the end of *Omeros*, he is thus able to teach Helen the deeper meaning of Boxing Day masquerades, which predate their Christmas associations.

The Battle of the Saints

Another line of Walcott's ancestral inheritance is through his European ancestors. This aspect of Caribbean history is largely enacted by Major Plunkett and his discovery of Midshipman Plunkett: men from separate centuries whose lives intersect after some two hundred years over a famous maritime battle between England and France. Walcott's treatment of the Battle of the Saints does not emphasize European glory. Dennis Plunkett is interested in this momentous battle for more domestic reasons. He and the poet see it as evidence of St. Lucia's intrinsic value, not as a European prize, but for its claim on them as individuals.

Compare & Contrast

- **1500s–1600s:** With the discovery of the West Indies, African slave trade begins along the Middle Passage bringing untold millions of Africans to the West Indies and the Americas.

  1800s: Millions of Africans and their descendants outnumber Anglo Europeans and their descendants in many areas of the New World. Plantation economy is based on slave labor. The American Civil War occurs between 1861 and 1865, taking the lives of 600,000 Americans and freeing an estimated four million slaves living in the United States.

Today: Legislations passed in the mid-twentieth century in the United States attempts to establish civil rights for all citizens, regardless of race, ethnicity, religion, or gender. Racial inequality persists into the early 2000s.

- **1500s–1600s:** Spain, Portugal, France, and England all colonize the West Indies and the Americas, bringing European diseases that decimate indigenous peoples.

1800s: Great Britain, France, and Belgium explore, map, and colonize the African continent, displacing and subjugating indigenous people and taking natural resources and exporting them. Anglo Americans move into the Texas area, establishing settlements and subjugating many local Hispanic peoples. Others move West, displacing Native Americans.

Today: The 1960s *Star Trek* series anticipates real-life exploration of outer space by space probes and cameras. Space stations provide experimentation bases for astronauts who live in space as long as six months or more.

- **1500s–1600s:** Arawaks have been supplanted by Caribs in the West Indies, but Caribs experience persistent decline in numbers with the advent of explorers and planters from Europe. As these Anglo Europeans settle in North and South America, indigenous people react in various ways, including expressions of welcome and resistance, and throughout the Americas, their populations drop because European diseases in the New World are fatal to indigenous people.

1800s: In 1830, the U.S. Congress passes the Indian Removal Act, which grants the president the power to order the resettlement of eastern tribes to areas west of the Mississippi River. In 1886, as the Statue of Liberty is erected in New York harbor, Geronimo surrenders. In 1890, the massacre at Wounded Knee in South Dakota occurs.

Today: Caribbean countries gain independence in the late twentieth century, and in the early 2000s, residents enjoy a parliamentary democracy and widespread literacy. However, unemployment is about 15 percent and poverty widespread. The

United States recognizes American Indian tribes as autonomous nations with their own jurisdictions.

- **1500s–1600s:** An agrarian lifestyle characterizes much of the known world; however, some tribes in the Americas are nomadic, following the flux of the seasons and migratory animals. As the use of slave labor increases in the New World, plantation economy develops. The economic and social differences between the small landed elite and the large labor force are dramatic.

1800s: Many sugar plantations in the West Indies use a large labor force. While slavery continues, the plantation economy thrives there and in the Americas, but inventions and resulting industrialization cause a proliferation of mills and factories, a rising middle class, and a cash-based economy in which increasingly people forego home production and purchase commodities from shops in town.

Today: Underdeveloped, so-called third world countries continue agrarian economies. Subsistence living among rural and urban populations makes extreme poverty common. Industrialized countries have diverse market economies and information technology grows at exponential rates.

Independence

For modern emancipated citizens of St. Lucia, such as Philoctete, Hector, and Maljo, the current battle to possess Helen centers on their social and political custodianship. Walcott witnessed the abortive experiment of the West Indian Federation from 1956 until its collapse in 1962. The failure of the Federation disappointed Walcott because he saw it as an opportunity to integrate the smaller islands into a more effective, stronger unit. In the aftermath of the Federation, St. Lucia became an independent state within the British Commonwealth on February 22, 1979. Although the federation does not figure directly in *Omeros*, the shortsightedness and political infighting that destroyed the Federation are embodied in the epic's national election scene. It is tempting to see in the acronyms of the two parties Maljo wishes to oppose the Progressive Labor Party (LP) and the United Workers' Party (UWP). The parallel is especially interesting since Walcott mentions a candidate named Compton and the Honorable John Compton of the United Workers' Party actually won the bitterly contested election of May 1982.

North and South

The shadow of North America looms large over the Caribbean basin and Walcott's professional life and is included in his West Indian epic. Walcott's participation in the poem as a persona, his insistence that he is a citizen of the Americas, and his sojourn to the United States, all make the States is as much a part of his extended landscape as Africa. Once again he telescopes history, this time to dramatize the irony of a postcolonial United States that nearly wiped out one race and enslaved another. Rather than focus on the genocidal policies that threaten to annihilate the Crow and Sioux, Walcott concentrates on the historical figure of Catherine Weldon, who lost a son and suffered the ostracism of her own race in order to support the Native American cause. Walcott gives a human face to sympathetic members of the white oppressor race, such as Weldon and the Plunketts, and in alluding to the many Western authors and artists in the Euro-American section of his epic, but he is not attempting to mitigate the evil of imperial domination and slavery; rather, he is attempting to come to grips with both the black and white polarities of his personal lineage and existence. The essential thrust of *Omeros* is reconciliation, redemption, and the empowerment of Creole West Indian consciousness.

Critical Overview

Prolific in his poetry and drama publications, with major contributions every decade from the 1940s into the early 2000s and with affiliations at prestigious universities in North America and Great Britain, Walcott is a critical success by any measure. The publication of *Omeros* in 1990 followed two years later by Walcott's receiving the Nobel Prize for literature confirmed what was already widely recognized: Walcott had proved himself to be a major twentieth-century poet. Moreover, his work came to prominence apace with and suited for the multicultural curricula popularized in the United States and critical interest in colonialism, post-colonialism, and the nature of the Other in art and literature. Plus, his handling of the epic literary canon in *Omeros* invited discussion of the (re)reading of major Western texts from the perspective of marginalized and dispossessed populations. By 2010, Walcott and his work were the subject of critical essays, book-length explications, and sophisticated biographical studies.

Regarding *Omeros* itself, many commentators first paid attention to Walcott's appropriation of classical epics. John Lucas, in a 1990 review for the *New Statesman and Society*, argued that Walcott's exploitation of the masters presents no constriction. Lucas went on to say that "the glory of *Omeros* is in the manner of its telling, in Walcott's masterly twining of the narrative threads, and also in the poem's seemingly inexhaustible linguistic riches." Rei Terada's 1992 book *Derek Walcott's Poetry: American Mimicry* stressed the complexity and sophistication of Walcott's manipulation of Homeric and other Western paradigms. Her chapter on *Omeros* developed the idea that Walcott disguises the representational nature of his own fictional characters by comparing them to their classical Greek archetypes. As a result, his "realistic" characters are more immediately vivified by being contrasted with the "art" they imitate.

Regarding the scope of *Omeros*, the verdict was divided. Quite a few reviewers suggested that Walcott was too ambitious and that he overwrote or spread this West Indian poem too thin in attempting to incorporate North America and Europe. But with reservations, Brad Leithauser, in the *New Yorker*, agreed with Lucas in praising Walcott's linguistic virtuosity. Adding to the discussion, St. Lucia-born scholar Pat Ismond, in her *Caribbean Contact* review, asserted that Walcott's poem is "informed by a lyric" rather than an epic muse. Furthermore, writing from her perspective within the Caribbean culture, Ismond disagreed with the metropolitan critics who found Walcott's excursions beyond the West Indies to be problematic. She praised the work's larger New World nexus of colonial reality. In confronting North America's unconscionable treatment of Native Americans, Ismond argued that Walcott "makes a truly revolutionary gesture," positing the heart of the United States in the Dakota plains rather than embracing the stereotypical image of Pilgrims in New England. Equally sensitive to the impetus behind Walcott's looking beyond the Caribbean, Geert Lernout argued in *Kunapipi* that it is the poet's dual vision that makes *Omeros* a "powerful achievement": "Walcott presents the two sides, the benevolent colonialism of the minor officials of the empire on the one hand and the descendants of slaves on the other."

The polarities noted by Lernout are also the sources of Walcott's personal and cultural heritage. The African episode in *Omeros* fits so seamlessly as to go unremarked by many critics. Creole by birth as well as by experience and education, Walcott knew his roots were nurtured by European as well as African sources. Lernout mentioned in passing that Walcott and James Joyce accomplish similarly patriotic objectives for their respective island nations. Writing for the *Southern Review*, Sidney Burris agreed. Burris insisted that in rhetoric, humor, structure and style, Joyce's *Ulysses* is likely to be the most important precursor to *Omeros.*

In addition to Homer and Joyce, critics found a growing number of telling parallels with other Western models. Several seized upon Helen as the thematic center of *Omeros*, making the case for Walcott's contribution to and extension of time-honored prototypes. According to Charlotte McClure in *Studies in the Literary Imagination*, Walcott's female protagonist assumes an identity of her own after 2,500 years of varied treatment. Comparing the Helens of Hart Crane and Hilda Doolittle with Walcott's creation, McClure concluded that without the benefit of female support within her patriarchal society, the Caribbean Helen achieves autonomy, ultimately breaking free of Homeric and Sophoclean associations. In *World Literature Today*, Julia Minkler drew upon Shakespeare's *Tempest* to discuss Helen among her St. Lucian Calibans, Prospero, Miranda Ariel, and Sycorax. Then, contributing to a collection entitled *Robinson Crusoe: Myths and Metamorphoses*, Paula Burnett located Walcott's new Helen within the rich Crusoe-Friday myth that itself grows out of the Ulysses legend. Due to their healing power, "moral courage, endurance, compassion, and knowledge of the human condition," Helen and Ma Kilman are primary forces in Walcott's narrative of the "handover of white power to black, in the name of a multiracial and multicultural future in which the wounds of history stay healed," Burnett wrote.

Even before Walcott's receipt of the Nobel Prize in 1992, *Omeros* began attracting serious scholarly attention. After that award, several more books on Walcott and his poem appeared, including Robert Hamner's *An Epic of the Dispossessed: Derek Walcott's Omeros* (1997); Patricia Ismond's *Abandoning Dead Metaphors: The Caribbean Phase of Derek Walcott's Poetry* (2002); and Lance Callahan's *In the Shadows of Divine Perfection: Derek Walcott's "Omeros"* (2003). At over 700 pages, Bruce King's *Derek Walcott: A Caribbean Life*, which was published by Oxford University Press in 2000, presents Walcott's biography in minute detail. From these critical responses, it is apparent that Walcott's *Omeros* was expected to sustain a weighty philosophical and aesthetic burden for years to come.

Sources

Bakken, Christopher, Review of *Omeros*, in *Georgia Review*, Vol. 45, No. 2, Summer 1991, pp. 403–406.

Bensen, Robert, "Catherine Weldon in *Omeros* and 'The Ghost Dance,'" in *Verse*, Vol. 22, No. 2, Summer 1994, pp. 119–25.

Brown, Robert, and Cheryl Johnson, "An Interview with Derek Walcott," in *Cream City Review*, Vol. 14, No. 2, Winter 1990, pp. 209–23.

Bruckner, D. J. R., "A Poem in Homage to an Unwanted Man," in *New York Times*, October 9, 1990, pp. 13, 17.

Burnett, Paula, "The Ulyssean Crusoe and the Quest for Redemption in J. M. Coetzee's *Foe* and Derek Walcott's *Omeros*," in *Robinson Crusoe: Myth and Metamorphoses*, edited by Lieve Spaas and Brian Stimpson, St. Martin's Press, 1996, pp. 239–55.

Ismond, Patricia, "Walcott's *Omeros*: A Complex, Ambitious Work," in *Caribbean Contact*, Vol. 18, No. 5, March—April 1991, pp. 10–11.

Kuh, Katherine, "Marcel Duchamp," in *The Artist's Voice: Talks with Seventeen Modern Artists*, Da Capo Press, 2000, pp. 81–93.

Lernout, Geert, "Derek Walcott's *Omeros*: The Isle Is Full of Voices," in *Kunapipi*, Vol. 14, No. 2, 1992, pp. 90–104.

Lucas, John, "The Sea, The Sea," in *New Statesman and Society*, Vol. 3, October 5, 1990, p. 36.

Mason, David, Review of *Omeros*, in *Hudson Review*, Vol. 44, No. 3, Fall 1991, pp. 513–15.

McClure, Charlotte S., "Helen of the 'West Indies': History or Poetry of a Caribbean Realm," in *Studies in the Literary Imagination*, Vol. 26, No. 2, Fall 1993, pp. 7–20.

O'Brien, Sean, "In Terms of the Ocean," in *Times Literary Supplement*, Vol. 4563, September 14–22, 1990, pp. 977–78.

Terada, Rei, "*Omeros*," in *Derek Walcott's Poetry: American Mimicry*, Northeastern University Press, 1992, pp. 183–227.

Walcott, Derek, *Omeros*, Farrar, Straus and Giroux, 1992.

White, J. P., "An Interview with Derek Walcott," in *Green Mountains Review*, New Series, Vol. 4, No. 1, Spring—Summer 1990, pp. 14–37.

Further Reading

Callahan, Lance, *In the Shadows of Divine Perfection: Derek Walcott's "Omeros,"* Studies in Major Literary Authors, Routledge, 2003.

> Callahan presents the first close reading of Walcott's epic, explaining the poem's Caribbean ideology with reference to Greek literature and culture and also criticizing postcolonial theory.

Hamner, Robert D., *Derek Walcott*, Twayne, 1993.

> In this work designed for students, Hamner examines Walcott's career up to his receipt of the Nobel Prize in 1992.

Hamner, Robert D., *Epic of the Dispossessed: Derek Walcott's "Omeros,"* University of Missouri Press, 1997.

> Hamner analyzes Walcott's epic both within the literary genre of which it is a part and as a distinct contradiction to the assumptions of works in that genre. He uses the term "dispossessed" because each of Walcott's characters are castaways and because the poet's voice comes from a marginalized, colonized site.

Hamner, Robert D., *"Omeros,"* in *The Cambridge*

Companion to the Epic, edited by Catherine Bates, Cambridge University Press, 2010.

> This essay examines Walcott's *Omeros* in terms of its adherence to and deviation from the epic genre. Whereas epics traditionally depend upon a cohesive national, racial, or spiritual framework, Walcott assembles his narrative against the New World's background of imperial exploitation and colonial neglect.

King, Bruce, *Derek Walcott: A Caribbean Life*, Oxford University Press, 2000.

This first-rate biography benefits from its author's friendship with the poet and access to a prose autobiography that remained unpublished as of 2000. King's massive study presents the social landscape and cultural background as a context for an intimate and respectful portrait of a complex man.

Kuh, Katherine, *The Artist's Voice: Talks with Seventeen Modern Artists*, Da Capo Press, 2000.

> One chapter of Kuh's book is devoted to Marcel Duchamp, whose experimental work, relying at times on accident, influenced Walcott in his conceptualizing a new way to write epic.

Walcott, Derek, *Another Life: Fully Annotated*, Lynne Rienner, 2004.

The Lynne Rienner edition of Walcott's book-length autobiographical poem, *Another Life*, provides the annotations readers need to appreciate both the work and the poet's life.

Suggested Search Terms

commonwealth literature

Derek Walcott

Derek Walcott AND colonialism

Derek Walcott AND Omeros

Greek epic

modern epic

Omeros

Omeros AND Odyssey

West Indian literature

Lightning Source UK Ltd.
Milton Keynes UK
UKHW021501210222
399002UK00010B/2614